Foreword

In a world characterized by rapid technological advancement, staying ahead of the curve is not merely an advantage; it's a necessity. As our lives become increasingly intertwined with artificial intelligence, it presents an opportunity—an opportunity to not only adapt but to thrive. And that's precisely what Max Riker's book, "Fast and Easy Ways to Make Money with AI," offers—a roadmap to harness the immense potential of AI for financial success.

Max Riker is no stranger to the transformative power of technology. With a background in both finance and AI, Max possesses a unique blend of expertise that enables him to navigate the complex intersection of money and machine intelligence. In this book, Max shares his insights, strategies, and the invaluable knowledge he's gained on the journey to financial prosperity through AI.

"Fast and Easy Ways to Make Money with AI" is not just another guide—it's a comprehensive manual that covers a wide spectrum of opportunities. From exploring the AI-driven financial markets to creating your own AI-powered ventures, Max leaves no stone unturned. Each chapter is a carefully crafted exploration into the vast landscape of possibilities, providing practical advice and real-world examples that will empower you to take action.

What makes this book truly exceptional is its focus on not only the 'how' but also the 'why.' Max Riker emphasizes the importance of aligning financial goals with ethical considerations, reminding us that in the pursuit of wealth, we have the power to contribute positively to society and the world at large.

In these pages, you'll discover how AI can be a force for good in your financial life, whether you're an investor, entrepreneur, freelancer, or someone seeking to elevate their career. Max's insights are delivered in a clear and accessible manner, making this book a valuable resource for both newcomers to AI and those already familiar with its potential.

As we venture deeper into the AI-driven future, Max Riker's book is a guiding light—a source of inspiration and actionable wisdom. It is my honor to introduce "Fast and Easy Ways to Make Money with AI" to you, dear reader. I encourage you to embrace the knowledge within these pages, for it has the potential to transform not only your financial prospects but also your perspective on the limitless possibilities that lie ahead.

Get ready to embark on a journey—a journey towards financial success, empowerment, and a brighter future. Max Riker is your trusted guide, and this book is your roadmap. May your path to prosperity with AI be fast, easy, and filled with meaningful rewards.

Chapter List:

Book Introduction:

In today's rapidly evolving world, artificial intelligence (AI) has emerged as a transformative force, revolutionizing the way we live, work, and do business. This groundbreaking technology has not only improved our lives but also opened up countless opportunities for financial success.

"Fast and Easy Ways to Make Money with AI" is your comprehensive guide to harnessing the power of AI for profit. Whether you're a seasoned entrepreneur or someone looking to dip their toes into the world of AI, this book will equip you with the knowledge and strategies to embark on a lucrative journey.

Over the course of these pages, we will explore the fundamental principles of AI, delve into its various applications across industries, and reveal innovative ways to leverage AI technologies for financial gain. From understanding the basics of AI to automating business processes, from tapping into the potential of AI in financial markets to creating AI-driven content that generates income, this book leaves no stone unturned.

But it's not all about profit. We'll also address the ethical considerations and risks associated with AI money-making ventures, ensuring that you navigate this exciting landscape responsibly and securely.

So, if you're ready to explore the world of AI money-making, fasten your seatbelt and prepare for a transformative journey. Let's dive into the first chapter and discover the foundations of this lucrative revolution.

In the grand scheme of technological advancements, few have had the profound impact that artificial intelligence (AI) has had in recent years. From self-driving cars to virtual personal assistants, AI has permeated every facet of our lives, making it smarter, more efficient, and yes, more profitable.

But what exactly is AI, and why is it causing such a buzz in the world of finance and business? In this first chapter, we'll embark on a journey of discovery, exploring the basics of AI and setting the stage for our exploration of its money-making potential.

Artificial intelligence refers to the development of computer systems that can perform tasks typically requiring human intelligence. These tasks include problem-solving, understanding natural language, recognizing patterns, and making decisions. In essence, AI systems are designed to mimic human cognitive functions, but often with greater speed and accuracy.

The roots of AI can be traced back to ancient history, where early inventors and philosophers dreamt of creating mechanical beings that could replicate human thought. However, it wasn't until the mid-20th century that AI as we know it today began to take shape. The term "artificial intelligence" was coined at the Dartmouth Conference in 1956, marking the official birth of the field.

From its humble beginnings, AI has come a long way. It now encompasses various subfields, including machine learning, natural language processing, computer vision, and robotics. Machine learning, in particular, has played a pivotal role in the recent AI renaissance. This approach involves training algorithms to learn from data and make predictions or decisions based on that learning. It's the driving force behind many AI applications we encounter daily, from recommendation systems on streaming platforms to predictive text on our smartphones.

AI's potential for profit lies in its ability to process vast amounts of data, identify patterns, and make predictions or automate tasks based on those patterns. This can lead to increased efficiency, reduced operational costs, and new revenue streams. Businesses across industries are waking up to the fact that AI is not just a technological novelty; it's a game-changer that can give them a competitive edge and drive financial success.

In the chapters that follow, we'll delve deeper into the specific ways AI is transforming industries and creating opportunities for individuals and organizations to make money. We'll explore machine learning, natural language processing, computer vision, and many other facets of AI, uncovering the strategies and tactics that can turn your AI-powered dreams into financial reality.

So, are you ready to embark on this exciting journey into the AI money-making revolution? Strap in, and let's explore the limitless possibilities that await you.

Chapter 2: Understanding the Basics of Artificial Intelligence

Now that we've laid the foundation in the first chapter by introducing AI and its significance, it's time to dive deeper into the fundamentals of artificial intelligence. Understanding these basics will equip you with the knowledge you need to navigate the intricate world of AI money-making.

At its core, AI seeks to replicate human intelligence using machines. But how does it do that? Let's break it down into a few key components:

1. Data: AI systems thrive on data. They learn from it, make decisions based on it, and become better over time. The more high-quality data you feed into an AI system, the more accurate and valuable its output becomes.

2. Algorithms: These are the mathematical instructions that govern how an AI system processes data. Algorithms are designed to perform specific tasks, from recognizing faces in images to predicting stock market trends.

3. Training: AI systems require training to learn from data. During this process, they adjust their internal parameters to optimize performance. Think of it as a machine learning from examples.

4. Inference: After training, AI systems can make predictions, decisions, or generate outputs based on new, unseen data. This is known as inference, and it's where AI becomes actionable.

5. Neural Networks: Neural networks are a type of AI architecture inspired by the human brain. They consist of interconnected nodes, or "neurons," that process and transmit information. Deep learning, a subset of machine learning, often uses deep neural networks for complex tasks.

6. Supervised vs. Unsupervised Learning: In supervised learning, AI models are trained on labeled data, where the correct answers are provided. In unsupervised learning, models find patterns and relationships in unlabeled data.

7. Reinforcement Learning: This is a type of machine learning where AI systems learn through trial and error, receiving rewards for making correct decisions and penalties for making mistakes.

Understanding these core elements will be invaluable as you explore the various ways AI can be applied to make money. In the subsequent chapters, we'll delve into specific AI applications and how they can be monetized.

Chapter 3: The Role of Machine Learning in Money-Making

Machine learning is the driving force behind many AI applications, and it's essential to grasp its significance in the AI money-making landscape. In this chapter, we'll explore the ins and outs of machine learning and its potential to generate revenue.

Machine learning is a subset of AI that focuses on the development of algorithms capable of learning from data. These algorithms adapt and improve their performance as they're exposed to more data, making them incredibly versatile and powerful.

Here are some key points to consider:

- Predictive Analytics: Machine learning models excel at predicting future outcomes based on historical data. This capability is invaluable in various industries, from finance (predicting stock prices) to marketing (forecasting customer behavior).
- Automation: Machine learning can automate repetitive tasks, freeing up human resources for more strategic activities. This not only increases efficiency but also reduces operational costs.
- Personalization: Many businesses use machine learning to personalize their offerings. Whether it's recommending products to shoppers or curating content for users, personalization can lead to increased sales and engagement.
- Anomaly Detection: Machine learning is adept at identifying anomalies or unusual patterns in data. In finance, for example, it can help detect fraudulent transactions or unusual market behavior.
- Natural Language Processing (NLP): NLP is a subset of machine learning that focuses on enabling computers to understand, interpret, and generate human language. NLP is

behind chatbots, sentiment analysis, and automated content generation.

As you explore the world of AI money-making, keep in mind that machine learning is not a one-size-fits-all solution. Success depends on choosing the right algorithms, collecting and preparing relevant data, and continually refining models.

In the chapters ahead, we'll examine specific applications of machine learning and how individuals and businesses can leverage this technology to create new revenue streams.

Chapter 4: Leveraging Natural Language Processing for Profit

Natural Language Processing (NLP) is a fascinating subfield of AI that focuses on enabling machines to understand, interpret, and generate human language. In this chapter, we'll explore how NLP can be a goldmine for profit generation.

NLP powers many applications you encounter daily:

- Chatbots and Virtual Assistants: These AI-powered entities can handle customer inquiries, provide support, and even make sales, all without human intervention.
- Sentiment Analysis: NLP can analyze text data (like social media posts or customer reviews) to gauge public sentiment. This insight is invaluable for businesses looking to improve their products and services.
- Content Generation: NLP models can generate human-like text, which can be used for everything from writing articles to creating marketing copy.
- Translation Services: NLP is behind the impressive strides made in machine translation, allowing businesses to reach global audiences more effectively.
- Search Engines: When you use a search engine, NLP helps match your query with relevant web pages.

NLP is particularly exciting because it bridges the gap between humans and machines, making interactions more natural and efficient. Whether you're looking to automate customer support, mine valuable insights from textual data, or even create content at scale, NLP can be a game-changer for your money-making endeavors.

In the following chapters, we'll delve deeper into specific NLP applications and strategies for monetizing them.

Chapter 5: Computer Vision: Seeing Opportunities Everywhere

In our exploration of the AI money-making landscape, we now turn our attention to computer vision, a field of artificial intelligence that empowers machines to see and interpret the visual world much like humans do. This chapter will shed light on the incredible potential of computer vision and how it can unlock opportunities for profit in various industries.

At its core, computer vision enables machines to process and understand visual information from the world around them. It involves capturing, analyzing, and making sense of images and videos. To achieve this, computer vision relies on a combination of hardware (like cameras and sensors) and sophisticated software, including deep learning algorithms.

Here are some key areas where computer vision is making a profound impact:

1. Object Detection and Recognition: Computer vision can identify and classify objects within images and videos. This capability has far-reaching applications, from autonomous vehicles recognizing pedestrians and other vehicles to retail stores automatically tracking inventory.

2. Facial Recognition: Facial recognition technology powered by computer vision can be used for security, authentication, and even personalized marketing. It's the technology behind unlocking your smartphone with your face.

3. Medical Imaging: Computer vision aids in the interpretation of medical images such as X-rays, MRIs, and CT scans. It assists healthcare professionals in diagnosing conditions and planning treatments.

4. Augmented Reality (AR) and Virtual Reality (VR): AR and VR experiences heavily rely on computer vision to overlay digital information onto the real world or immerse users in virtual environments.

5. Industrial Automation: In manufacturing, computer vision can inspect products for defects, guide robots in assembly processes, and monitor equipment for maintenance needs.

6. Agriculture: Computer vision is used to monitor crop health, identify pests and diseases, and optimize farming practices.

7. Retail: Retailers employ computer vision for shelf monitoring, customer analytics, and cashier-less stores where shoppers can grab items and leave without going through a traditional checkout process.

The potential for profit in these areas is substantial. For entrepreneurs and businesses, understanding how to harness computer vision can lead to efficiency improvements, cost reductions, and the development of innovative products and services.

As we progress through this book, we will delve deeper into specific applications of computer vision and uncover strategies for turning this visual perception into financial gain. Computer vision is not just about seeing; it's about seeing opportunities everywhere you look.

Chapter 6: Recommender Systems: Personalized Profit Generation

In the digital age, where information overload is a constant challenge, recommender systems have emerged as a powerful tool for both consumers and businesses. This chapter explores how recommender systems, a subset of artificial intelligence, can be harnessed for personalized profit generation.

Recommender systems, often referred to as recommendation engines, are AI algorithms that provide personalized suggestions to users. These suggestions can range from product recommendations on e-commerce platforms to movie and music recommendations on streaming services. The goal is to enhance user experience, drive engagement, and, most importantly, boost revenue.

Here's how recommender systems work:

1. Data Collection: Recommender systems collect data on user behavior and preferences. This can include past purchases, items viewed, ratings given, and even demographic information.

2. Data Analysis: AI algorithms analyze this data to identify patterns and relationships. For example, they might notice that users who bought a particular book also tend to purchase certain related items.

3. Personalization: Based on the analysis, the recommender system generates personalized recommendations for each user. These recommendations can be in the form of product suggestions, content recommendations, or even advertising.

4. Feedback Loop: As users interact with the recommendations (e.g., making purchases or providing feedback), the system continues to learn and refine its suggestions. It adapts to changing preferences and behaviors.

Recommender systems have become ubiquitous, and you've likely encountered them on platforms like Amazon, Netflix, Spotify, and social media sites. These systems not only enhance user satisfaction but also play a pivotal role in revenue generation. Here's how:

1. Increased Sales: By suggesting products or services tailored to a user's interests, recommender systems can significantly boost sales. When customers feel that a platform understands their preferences, they're more likely to make purchases.

2. Improved User Engagement: Personalized recommendations keep users engaged and coming back for more. This increases user retention and the potential for repeat business.

3. Cross-Selling and Up-Selling: Recommender systems can suggest complementary or higher-priced items, increasing the average transaction value.

4. Advertising Revenue: Platforms can monetize their recommendation systems by promoting sponsored products or ads that align with a user's interests.

5. Reduced Decision Fatigue: In a world with abundant choices, recommender systems simplify decision-making, reducing the cognitive load on users and increasing their likelihood to make a purchase.

Whether you're a business owner, content creator, or marketer, understanding how to leverage recommender systems for personalized profit generation is crucial in today's competitive landscape. In the chapters that follow, we'll explore real-world examples and strategies to make the most of recommender systems and create a win-win scenario for both you and your customers. Personalization is not just a trend; it's a potent revenue-generating tool.

Chapter 7: AI in Financial Markets: A Goldmine of Opportunities

Financial markets have always been a hotbed of activity, driven by the constant pursuit of profit. In recent years, the integration of artificial intelligence (AI) into the financial sector has ushered in a new era of opportunity and innovation. This chapter explores how AI is revolutionizing financial markets and how individuals and institutions can tap into this goldmine of opportunities.

The Power of AI in Finance:

AI technologies, particularly machine learning, have found fertile ground in the financial world. Here's how AI is transforming the landscape:

Algorithmic Trading: AI-powered algorithms analyze market data at lightning speed, identifying trading opportunities and executing trades far more efficiently than human traders. These algorithms can handle vast volumes of data and adapt to changing market conditions in real-time.

Risk Management: AI models can assess risk with unprecedented accuracy. They analyze historical data, market sentiment, and news feeds to predict potential risks and suggest risk mitigation strategies.

Fraud Detection: AI is instrumental in detecting fraudulent transactions in real-time. It can identify unusual patterns and flag suspicious activity, protecting both financial institutions and their customers.

Customer Service: Chatbots and virtual assistants powered by AI provide instant customer support, answer queries, and even help with financial planning.

Portfolio Management: Robo-advisors use AI to create and manage investment portfolios based on individual goals and risk tolerance, often with lower fees than traditional financial advisors.

Credit Scoring: AI-driven credit scoring models can assess creditworthiness more accurately by considering a broader range of data points beyond traditional credit scores.

AI and Profit Potential:

The application of AI in finance offers several pathways to profit:

- Trading: High-frequency trading and quantitative strategies can generate substantial returns, but they require expertise and careful risk management.
- Fintech Startups: Entrepreneurs can create AI-powered fintech solutions to address specific market needs, such as peer-to-peer lending platforms, investment apps, or digital banks.
- Investment: Individual investors can use AI-powered tools to make informed investment decisions and manage their portfolios more effectively.
- Data Analytics: AI-driven data analytics can uncover insights that inform investment strategies, risk management, and market analysis.
- Consulting and Services: Professionals with AI expertise can offer consulting services to financial institutions seeking to implement AI solutions.

As you venture into AI-driven financial markets, remember that the landscape is both promising and complex. Success requires a deep understanding of finance, robust AI skills, and a commitment to staying updated with evolving regulations.

In the chapters ahead, we'll delve into specific AI applications in finance, explore case studies of successful AI-driven financial ventures, and provide guidance on how to navigate this dynamic and lucrative field. AI is reshaping finance, and those who embrace it can unlock a world of financial opportunities.

Chapter 8: Automating Business Processes with AI

The rapid advancement of artificial intelligence (AI) has ushered in a new era of business process automation. From streamlining routine tasks to optimizing complex workflows, AI is transforming the way organizations operate. In this chapter, we'll explore how businesses of all sizes can leverage AI to automate processes, improve efficiency, and ultimately boost profitability.

The Power of AI in Automation:

AI-driven automation offers several advantages for businesses:

> Cost Savings: By automating repetitive tasks, businesses can significantly reduce labor costs and improve operational efficiency.
> Error Reduction: AI systems are less prone to human errors, leading to higher accuracy in tasks such as data entry, document processing, and quality control.
> Speed and Scalability: AI-powered automation can complete tasks at a much faster pace than humans and can easily scale up to handle increasing workloads.
> Data Analysis: AI algorithms can process vast amounts of data to provide valuable insights for decision-making, customer segmentation, and market analysis.
> Enhanced Customer Experience: Chatbots and virtual assistants offer round-the-clock customer support, improving response times and user satisfaction.

Key Areas of AI-Driven Automation:

Businesses can apply AI-driven automation across various domains:

Customer Support: Chatbots and AI-powered virtual assistants can handle customer inquiries, provide product recommendations, and assist with troubleshooting.

Finance and Accounting: Automation can streamline invoice processing, expense tracking, and financial reporting, reducing the workload for finance teams.

Human Resources: AI can assist in candidate screening, employee onboarding, and benefits administration.

Supply Chain Management: AI can optimize inventory management, demand forecasting, and logistics, leading to cost savings and improved delivery times.

Marketing and Sales: AI-driven marketing automation tools can personalize marketing campaigns, lead scoring, and customer engagement.

Quality Control: AI-powered image recognition and quality control systems can identify defects in manufacturing processes.

Legal and Compliance: AI can assist in contract analysis, patent searches, and regulatory compliance monitoring.

Implementing AI Automation:

To harness the potential of AI-driven automation, businesses should follow a structured approach:

Identify Automation Opportunities: Assess your business processes to identify tasks that are repetitive, rule-based, and suitable for automation.

Select the Right AI Tools: Choose AI solutions that align with your automation goals. This may involve implementing off-the-shelf software or developing custom AI applications.

Data Integration: Ensure that data from various sources can be integrated into the AI system for analysis and decision-making.

Testing and Training: Thoroughly test and train your AI system to ensure it performs effectively and aligns with business objectives.
Monitoring and Optimization: Continuously monitor the performance of your AI automation, identify bottlenecks or errors, and make improvements accordingly.

Case Studies and Success Stories:

Throughout this chapter, we'll explore real-world case studies and success stories of businesses that have successfully implemented AI-driven automation to streamline their operations, reduce costs, and enhance customer experiences.

AI-driven automation is not limited to large enterprises. Small and medium-sized businesses can also benefit by selectively implementing AI solutions to improve efficiency and competitiveness. As we delve into practical applications and strategies in the chapters ahead, you'll gain valuable insights into how AI can be a game-changer in automating your business processes and driving profitability.

Chapter 9: AI-Powered E-commerce: A Shopper's Paradise

E-commerce has evolved into a booming industry, reshaping the way we shop and do business. The integration of artificial intelligence (AI) has played a pivotal role in this transformation, offering a personalized and efficient shopping experience for consumers while opening up lucrative opportunities for online retailers. In this chapter, we'll explore how AI is shaping the e-commerce landscape and how businesses can harness its power to thrive in this digital shopping paradise.

The AI Revolution in E-commerce:

Artificial intelligence has revolutionized various aspects of the e-commerce ecosystem:

> Personalization: AI algorithms analyze customer behavior and preferences to provide personalized product recommendations, increasing the likelihood of conversions and repeat purchases.
>
> Search and Discovery: AI-powered search engines and chatbots understand natural language queries, helping shoppers find products more easily and enhancing the user experience.
>
> Inventory Management: AI optimizes inventory levels, reducing stockouts and overstock situations while maximizing profitability.
>
> Pricing Optimization: Dynamic pricing algorithms adjust prices based on real-time market conditions, competitor pricing, and demand, ensuring competitive yet profitable pricing strategies.
>
> Customer Service: Chatbots and virtual assistants offer 24/7 support, answering queries, providing product information, and facilitating seamless transactions.

AI-Powered E-commerce Strategies:

For businesses in the e-commerce sector, here are some strategies to leverage AI effectively:

> Personalization: Implement AI-driven recommendation engines to provide personalized product suggestions based on customer behavior and preferences.
> Chatbots and Virtual Assistants: Integrate chatbots and virtual assistants to improve customer support, answer inquiries, and guide users through the purchase process.
> Visual Search: Utilize AI to enable visual search, allowing customers to find products by uploading images, which can be especially useful for fashion and home decor e-commerce.
> Dynamic Pricing: Deploy dynamic pricing algorithms to remain competitive while maximizing profits. Monitor market trends and competitor pricing to adjust prices in real-time.
> Inventory Optimization: Use AI to forecast demand accurately, reduce excess inventory, and ensure product availability.
> Fraud Detection: Implement AI-driven fraud detection systems to protect against online payment fraud and maintain the trust of your customers.

Enhancing the Customer Journey:

AI has the power to enhance every step of the customer journey in e-commerce:

> Discovery: AI helps customers discover products tailored to their tastes through personalized recommendations and intuitive search interfaces.

Decision-Making: Dynamic pricing and detailed product information assist customers in making informed purchase decisions.

Transaction: Chatbots and virtual assistants simplify the transaction process, making it seamless and efficient.

Post-Purchase: AI can follow up with personalized recommendations, order tracking, and customer support, ensuring a positive post-purchase experience.

The Future of E-commerce with AI:

As AI technology continues to advance, e-commerce will witness even more transformative changes. Emerging trends include:

Voice Commerce: AI-powered voice assistants enable voice-activated shopping, making purchases as simple as speaking a command.

Augmented Reality (AR) Shopping: AR applications allow customers to visualize products in their environment before purchasing, such as trying on virtual clothing or placing furniture in their homes.

AI-Enhanced Customer Insights: Deeper insights into customer behavior will enable more precise targeting and personalization.

Supply Chain Optimization: AI-driven predictive analytics will enhance supply chain management, reducing delivery times and costs.

AI is ushering in an era of unprecedented convenience and personalization in e-commerce. Whether you're an established online retailer or an aspiring entrepreneur, understanding and harnessing the power of AI is essential to thriving in this shopper's paradise. In the chapters ahead, we'll delve into real-world examples and practical strategies to help you navigate the dynamic world of AI-powered e-commerce successfully.

Chapter 10: Monetizing Data: Turning Information into Income

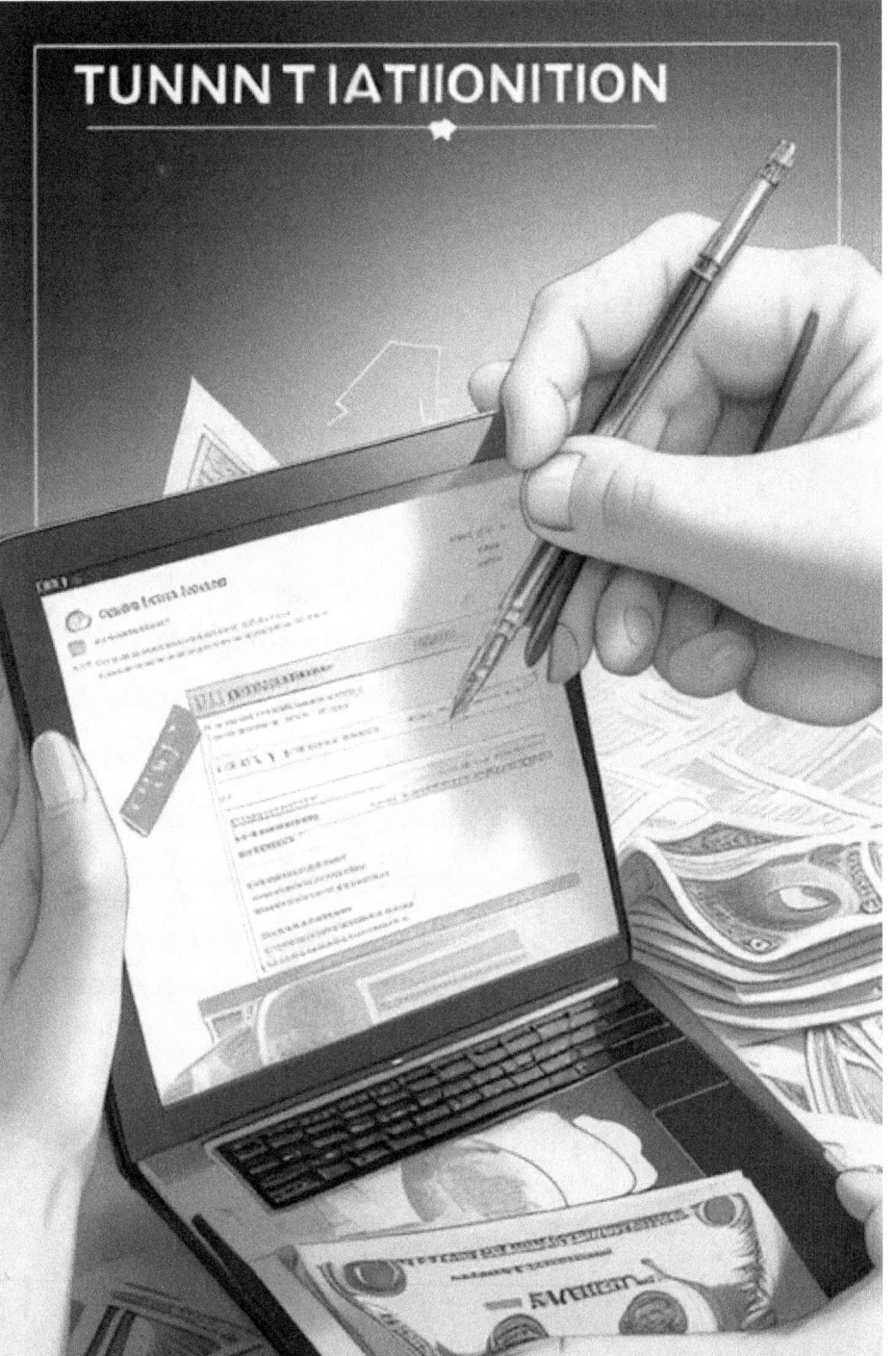

In the digital age, data has become one of the most valuable assets for businesses and individuals alike. The ability to collect, analyze, and leverage data effectively can be a significant source of income. In this chapter, we will explore how to monetize data, whether you're a business looking to capitalize on your data assets or an individual seeking opportunities in the data-driven economy.

The Data Revolution:

Data is generated at an astonishing rate, thanks to the proliferation of digital devices, social media, e-commerce, and the Internet of Things (IoT). This data deluge has opened up diverse opportunities for monetization:

Data Selling: Businesses can sell their data to other organizations, providing valuable insights for marketing, research, and decision-making.

Data Analytics Services: Offer data analytics services to businesses looking to extract insights from their data but lacking the necessary expertise.

Data-Driven Products: Develop data-driven products and services, such as recommendation engines, market insights, or predictive analytics tools.

Data-Enhanced Content: Content creators can use data to inform and enhance their content, catering to specific audiences and increasing engagement.

Data Marketplaces: Join data marketplaces where individuals and organizations can buy and sell data sets, algorithms, or models.

Monetization Strategies:

For businesses and individuals looking to monetize data, consider these strategies:

Identify Valuable Data: Determine which data you possess is valuable and relevant to others. This might include customer behavior, market trends, or niche expertise.

Data Quality: Ensure that your data is accurate, up-to-date, and properly cleaned to maximize its value.

Privacy and Compliance: Be aware of data privacy regulations, such as GDPR or CCPA, and ensure that your data collection and sharing practices comply with these laws.

Data Licensing: When selling data, consider different licensing models, such as one-time sales, subscriptions, or usage-based pricing.

Data Security: Protect the data you collect and share. Data breaches can have severe financial and reputational consequences.

Market Research: Understand your target audience and the market demand for the data you offer. Conduct market research to set competitive prices.

Case Studies and Success Stories:

Throughout this chapter, we'll delve into real-world case studies and success stories of individuals and organizations that have effectively monetized their data assets. These stories will provide valuable insights and inspiration for your own data monetization journey.

Individual Opportunities:

Individuals can also tap into the data economy:

Data Collection Apps: Use apps and devices that allow you to collect data on various aspects of your life, from health and fitness to consumer preferences.

Participate in Surveys: Participate in market research surveys and data collection initiatives that offer compensation.

Content Monetization: If you create content, leverage data to tailor your content to your audience's interests and maximize engagement.

Freelance Data Analysis: Offer freelance data analysis services to businesses or organizations in need of data expertise.

The data economy is expanding, and the potential for monetization is vast. Whether you're a business looking to capitalize on your data assets or an individual interested in participating in the data-driven economy, the opportunities are abundant. As you progress through this chapter, you'll gain valuable insights and practical strategies for turning information into income.

Chapter 11: The Gig Economy and AI: Creating Income Independence

The gig economy has revolutionized the way people work and generate income. With the integration of artificial intelligence (AI), individuals can tap into a vast array of opportunities to secure income independence and thrive in this dynamic landscape. In this chapter, we'll explore how AI is reshaping the gig economy and how you can harness its power to create a sustainable income stream.

The Gig Economy Unleashed:

The gig economy, characterized by short-term contracts, freelance work, and independent employment, has witnessed remarkable growth in recent years. It offers several advantages, including flexibility, autonomy, and income diversification. AI is a driving force behind the gig economy's expansion:

> Matching Platforms: AI-powered platforms connect gig workers with job opportunities that align with their skills and preferences, optimizing the job market.
> Task Automation: AI automates repetitive tasks, allowing gig workers to focus on higher-value activities and increasing productivity.
> Predictive Analytics: AI analyzes market trends, demand patterns, and pricing dynamics, helping gig workers make informed decisions and maximize their earning potential.
> Personalized Services: AI enables gig workers to provide personalized services to clients, enhancing customer satisfaction and repeat business.

Leveraging AI in the Gig Economy:

For individuals looking to thrive in the gig economy with the help of AI, consider these strategies:

Skill Development: Acquire AI-relevant skills and expertise to remain competitive in the gig job market. This may include data analysis, machine learning, or AI programming.
Platform Utilization: Leverage AI-powered gig platforms to find job opportunities that match your skills and interests. These platforms often use AI algorithms for job matching.
AI Tools and Automation: Use AI tools to automate tasks, streamline your workflow, and enhance your productivity.
Market Insights: Utilize AI-driven market insights to make data-informed decisions, such as setting pricing strategies or choosing in-demand gig categories.
Collaboration with AI: Embrace collaboration with AI systems that can enhance your capabilities, whether it's chatbots handling customer inquiries or AI-generated content.

Case Studies and Success Stories:

Throughout this chapter, we'll delve into real-world case studies and success stories of individuals who have harnessed AI in the gig economy. These stories will provide inspiration and practical insights into how AI can be a game-changer in achieving income independence.

AI and the Future of Work:

As AI technology continues to advance, the gig economy will evolve as well. Emerging trends include:

AI-Enhanced Services: Gig workers may collaborate closely with AI systems to provide more sophisticated and personalized services.

Global Opportunities: AI-powered platforms will facilitate global gig opportunities, allowing workers to access a broader client base.

AI Entrepreneurship: AI enables individuals to create their own gig platforms or businesses, catering to specific niches and markets.

Skill Augmentation: AI may be used to augment workers' skills, making them more versatile and adaptable to a changing job landscape.

The gig economy, coupled with AI, offers unprecedented opportunities for income independence and professional growth. Whether you're a freelancer, independent contractor, or aspiring gig worker, understanding and harnessing the power of AI is essential to thriving in this evolving landscape. In the chapters ahead, you'll gain valuable insights and practical strategies for achieving income independence in the gig economy.

Chapter 12: AI and Education: Learning and Earning in the Digital Age

Education has always been a pathway to personal growth and career success. In today's digital age, the integration of artificial intelligence (AI) is revolutionizing the way we learn and, consequently, how we earn. In this chapter, we'll explore how AI is transforming education and creating opportunities for individuals to acquire new skills, enhance their careers, and increase their earning potential.

The AI Revolution in Education:

AI has brought about significant changes in the education sector, impacting both traditional and online learning. Here are some key ways in which AI is transforming education:

Personalized Learning: AI-powered educational platforms analyze students' strengths and weaknesses, tailoring learning materials and pacing to individual needs.

Automated Grading: AI can assess assignments, tests, and even essays, providing immediate feedback to students and reducing the workload on educators.

Language Learning: AI-driven language apps and platforms offer personalized language learning experiences, enabling users to acquire new languages more efficiently.

Skill Development: AI-powered skill-based platforms provide opportunities for individuals to acquire in-demand skills, often with certifications or micro-credentials.

Content Creation: AI-generated content and lessons can supplement educational materials, offering a variety of perspectives and learning resources.

Learning and Earning with AI:

For individuals looking to leverage AI in their educational journey for career advancement and increased income, consider these strategies:

Skill Enhancement: Identify the skills that are in demand in your industry or desired career path. Seek out AI-powered learning platforms that offer courses or programs in these areas.

Certifications and Credentials: Many AI-powered educational platforms offer certifications or micro-credentials upon course completion. These credentials can enhance your resume and earning potential.

Professional Networking: Join online communities and networks related to your field of interest. AI can facilitate connections with professionals and mentors who can guide your career growth.

AI Career Advisors: AI-driven career advisory tools can provide insights into job market trends, salary expectations, and career growth opportunities.

Lifelong Learning: Embrace a mindset of lifelong learning. AI enables you to continually update your skills and knowledge throughout your career.

Case Studies and Success Stories:

Throughout this chapter, we'll delve into real-world case studies and success stories of individuals who have used AI in their education to enhance their careers and earning potential. These stories will provide inspiration and practical insights into how AI can be a catalyst for personal and professional growth.

AI and the Future of Learning:

As AI technology continues to advance, the future of education will see further transformations:

> AI-Powered Mentorship: AI-driven mentorship programs will offer personalized guidance and career advice to learners.
> Virtual Labs: AI-driven virtual labs and simulations will enhance experiential learning in fields like science and engineering.
> AI-Enhanced Curriculum: Educational institutions will increasingly integrate AI into their curricula, preparing students for AI-powered workplaces.
> Global Learning: AI will enable learners to access educational content and opportunities from around the world, fostering global perspectives and competencies.

Education has always been a key driver of career success, and AI is amplifying its impact. Whether you're a student, a working professional, or someone looking to pivot into a new career, understanding and harnessing the power of AI in education can be the catalyst for personal and professional growth, ultimately leading to increased earning potential in the digital age. In the chapters ahead, you'll gain valuable insights and practical strategies for leveraging AI in your educational and career journey.

Chapter 13: AI in Healthcare: Healing and Earning

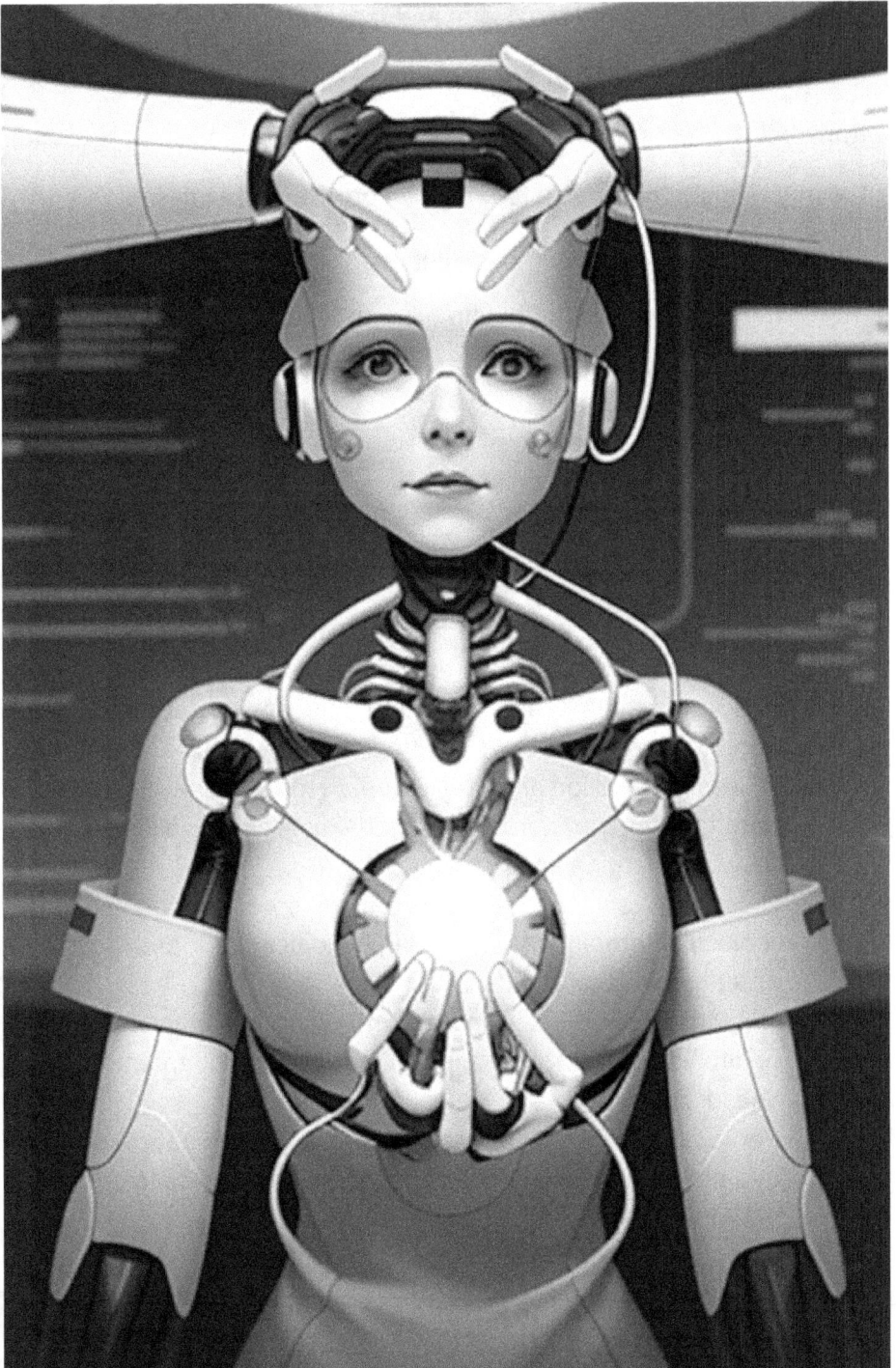

Healthcare is one of the most vital and rapidly evolving industries globally. The integration of artificial intelligence (AI) has brought about transformative changes in patient care, diagnostics, research, and even the potential for individuals to create income opportunities. In this chapter, we'll explore how AI is reshaping healthcare and the ways it can be leveraged for both better health outcomes and financial gain.

AI's Impact on Healthcare:

AI has made significant inroads in healthcare, and its applications are wide-ranging:

> Medical Imaging: AI-powered algorithms can analyze medical images, such as X-rays, MRIs, and CT scans, to detect abnormalities and assist radiologists in diagnosis.
> Disease Prediction and Prevention: AI models analyze patient data to identify patterns and predict disease risk, allowing for early intervention and prevention.
> Drug Discovery: AI accelerates drug discovery by simulating molecular interactions, analyzing biological data, and identifying potential drug candidates.
> Healthcare Chatbots: Chatbots and virtual assistants offer 24/7 health advice, symptom assessment, and appointment scheduling.
> Personalized Treatment Plans: AI can analyze a patient's genetics, medical history, and real-time health data to create personalized treatment plans.

Healthcare and Income Generation:

For individuals looking to leverage AI for financial opportunities within the healthcare sector, consider the following strategies:

Health Data Monetization: Explore platforms and services that allow you to monetize your health data, with your consent, for medical research or clinical trials.

Health Tech Entrepreneurship: If you have a background in healthcare or AI, consider starting a health tech company. Develop AI-driven solutions that address specific healthcare challenges.

Telemedicine Services: Offer telemedicine services or virtual health consultations using AI-powered chatbots or platforms.

AI Health Consulting: Become an AI health consultant, providing expertise to healthcare institutions or businesses looking to implement AI solutions.

Medical Data Analysis: If you have the necessary skills, offer medical data analysis services to healthcare providers, researchers, or pharmaceutical companies.

Case Studies and Success Stories:

Throughout this chapter, we'll delve into real-world case studies and success stories of individuals who have successfully integrated AI into healthcare, whether through entrepreneurship, data monetization, or consulting. These stories will provide inspiration and practical insights into how AI can be a game-changer in healthcare and income generation.

AI and the Future of Healthcare:

As AI continues to advance, healthcare will see even more transformative changes:

AI-Enhanced Diagnostics: AI will play an increasingly central role in diagnosing diseases and recommending treatment options.
Remote Monitoring: AI-powered wearables and devices will enable continuous health monitoring, facilitating early intervention and personalized care.
Drug Development: AI-driven drug discovery will lead to more efficient development processes and personalized medicine.
AI-Integrated Clinics: Healthcare facilities will integrate AI into their workflows, improving efficiency and patient care.
AI-Assisted Surgery: AI-powered robotic surgery systems will become more commonplace, enhancing surgical precision and reducing recovery times.

The convergence of AI and healthcare presents unprecedented opportunities for individuals to contribute to better health outcomes while also creating income streams. Whether you have a healthcare background, technical skills, or an interest in health tech entrepreneurship, understanding and harnessing the power of AI in healthcare can lead to both improved health and financial rewards. In the chapters ahead, you'll gain valuable insights and practical strategies for navigating the evolving landscape of AI in healthcare.

Chapter 14: AI and Sustainability: Profits with a Purpose

In an era marked by environmental challenges and a growing commitment to sustainability, artificial intelligence (AI) is emerging as a powerful force for both profit generation and environmental responsibility. In this chapter, we'll explore how AI is revolutionizing sustainability efforts and how businesses and individuals can align their financial goals with a commitment to a more sustainable future.

AI's Role in Sustainability:

AI is playing a pivotal role in advancing sustainability across various domains:

> Energy Efficiency: AI-driven systems can optimize energy consumption in buildings, industrial processes, and transportation, reducing waste and costs.
> Climate Modeling: AI models analyze vast climate data sets to improve climate change predictions and guide mitigation efforts.
> Agricultural Sustainability: AI assists farmers in precision agriculture, optimizing resource use and reducing environmental impacts.
> Waste Reduction: AI can streamline recycling processes, identify opportunities for waste reduction, and improve waste management.
> Conservation: AI-powered monitoring systems track wildlife populations, protect endangered species, and combat illegal poaching.

Profits with a Purpose:

For businesses and individuals looking to align profit generation with sustainability goals, consider these strategies:

Green Technology: Develop or invest in AI-driven green technologies that address environmental challenges, such as renewable energy solutions or pollution reduction systems.

Sustainable Supply Chains: Use AI to optimize supply chain operations, reducing waste, energy consumption, and emissions.

Environmental Data Analytics: Offer AI-driven environmental data analysis services to businesses, governments, or nonprofits looking to enhance their sustainability efforts.

Green Investments: Invest in companies and startups that prioritize sustainability and AI-driven solutions for environmental challenges.

Sustainable Marketing: Highlight your commitment to sustainability in your marketing and branding efforts, appealing to eco-conscious consumers.

Case Studies and Success Stories:

Throughout this chapter, we'll delve into real-world case studies and success stories of businesses and individuals who have successfully integrated AI into their sustainability efforts, demonstrating that profits and sustainability can go hand in hand.

AI and the Future of Sustainability:

As AI technology continues to advance, sustainability efforts will become increasingly AI-driven:

Carbon Reduction: AI will play a central role in optimizing carbon capture, storage, and reduction technologies.

Environmental Monitoring: AI-driven Earth-observing satellites and drones will provide real-time data for environmental monitoring and disaster management.

Circular Economy: AI will facilitate the transition to a circular economy by optimizing recycling and reuse processes.

Consumer Engagement: AI-powered apps and platforms will empower consumers to make environmentally responsible choices in their daily lives.

Eco-Friendly Transportation: AI will drive the development of eco-friendly transportation solutions, from electric and autonomous vehicles to efficient public transportation systems.

The intersection of AI and sustainability offers opportunities for individuals and businesses to not only generate profits but also contribute to a more sustainable and environmentally responsible future. Whether you're an entrepreneur, investor, or professional in any field, understanding and harnessing the power of AI in sustainability can be a catalyst for both financial success and positive environmental impact. In the chapters ahead, you'll gain valuable insights and practical strategies for navigating the dynamic landscape of AI-driven sustainability

Chapter 15: AI and Personal Finance: Smart Strategies for Wealth

Personal finance is a topic of universal importance, and artificial intelligence (AI) is rapidly becoming a key player in helping individuals make informed financial decisions, manage their wealth, and secure their financial future. In this final chapter, we'll explore how AI is transforming personal finance and how you can harness its power to build wealth, achieve financial goals, and secure a prosperous future.

AI's Impact on Personal Finance:

AI has ushered in a new era of personal finance, with applications that include:

> Financial Planning: AI-powered financial advisors create personalized financial plans, considering income, expenses, investments, and goals.
> Investment Management: Robo-advisors use AI algorithms to manage investment portfolios, optimizing asset allocation and risk management.
> Expense Tracking: AI-driven budgeting apps track spending patterns, identify areas for savings, and provide real-time financial insights.
> Credit and Loans: AI assesses creditworthiness and helps individuals secure loans and credit at favorable terms.
> Fraud Prevention: AI detects and prevents fraudulent transactions, safeguarding individuals' financial assets.

Wealth-Building Strategies with AI:

For individuals looking to leverage AI for personal finance and wealth-building, consider these strategies:

Robo-Advisory Services: Invest in robo-advisory platforms that use AI to manage your investment portfolio, aligning it with your financial goals and risk tolerance.

Budgeting and Expense Apps: Use AI-driven budgeting apps that provide real-time insights into your spending habits and suggest ways to save money.

AI Credit Tools: Utilize AI-powered credit score improvement services that offer tailored advice to boost your creditworthiness.

AI-Enhanced Savings: Explore AI-driven savings accounts that optimize your savings strategy, earning you the highest interest rates available.

Automated Investments: Set up automated investment plans that use AI to make regular contributions to your portfolio.

Case Studies and Success Stories:

Throughout this chapter, we'll delve into real-world case studies and success stories of individuals who have successfully integrated AI into their personal finance strategies, achieving financial security and wealth accumulation.

AI and the Future of Personal Finance:

As AI technology continues to advance, personal finance will see further innovations:

Hyper-Personalization: AI will provide even more personalized financial advice, considering an individual's unique financial situation and goals.

Enhanced Financial Literacy: AI-driven educational tools will help individuals improve their financial literacy, making informed decisions.

Predictive Analytics: AI will use predictive analytics to forecast financial trends, helping individuals make proactive financial decisions.

Risk Management: AI will offer sophisticated risk management tools, ensuring that investments align with an individual's risk tolerance.

Blockchain and Cryptocurrencies: AI-driven solutions will facilitate the management of blockchain assets and cryptocurrencies, offering secure and efficient investment options.

In the rapidly evolving landscape of personal finance, AI is a powerful ally for individuals seeking to build wealth, achieve financial goals, and secure their financial future. Whether you're just starting your financial journey or looking to optimize your existing strategies, understanding and harnessing the power of AI in personal finance can be a game-changer. In the chapters ahead, you'll gain valuable insights and practical strategies to navigate the dynamic world of AI-driven personal finance.

www.ingramcontent.com/pod-product-compliance
Lightning Source LLC
Chambersburg PA
CBHW062254290526
45794CB00006B/2548